The Neon Rosary

ekphrases in tiny prose poems

by Lorette C. Luzajic

with love, for Paulo, a true friend and queen of
all that sparkles

Contents

The Neon Rosary

after *Seven,* by William Wray (USA) contemporary

I tell you I am drowning in my pictures, how the colours are closing in around me. I tell you the moon has tumbled out of the darkness and is spitting pale tongues of flame, like rosary beads, from the O in *hotel* in an old neon sign.

Las Ramblas

after *Plaza Real,* by Costa Vila (Spain) contemporary

It rained that day, and you were tired and you were never tired, so we hailed a cab back to our Air BnB room. You took everything off and you never nap naked, crawled to stark sleep under a single sheet. Barcelona has a way of getting under your skin. The art, the fish, the wine. It was an old world covered in spiraling rainbows of broken pottery, and ceilings hanged with Spanish jamon. The spirits were everywhere.

After awhile you stirred the way you always did if there was a shift in the room. Why are you crying? you asked and your voice was soft with sleep. Oh, I'm not crying, I said. You nodded. It's only everything, I said. I knew you understood how I cried all the time. How I got so filled up with beauty, I had to release a bit of sea to get back to earth.

Rare Bones

after *City,* by Joso Spralja (Canada, b. Croatia) c. 1970s

Walled city, sea without end. Venus struts boardwalk with violin. Troubadours roam these streets, conjured in the solitudes that spanned the centuries before I was dreamed into breath. The red roofs, the spires, the absence of their shadows. Only the waves held the sun.

Jehovah's Witness

after *Homeless,* by Fernand Pelez (France) 1883

Jesus, alabaster, white as snow before his onlooker's mullet and maraschino crocs. Beneath the concave abdomen, and at the Saviour's feet, the stranger genuflects, takes a handful of milagros from a paper sack and scatters them like seeds. *I see you, Jesus,* he says. *Do you see me?*

Vanadium

after *Violet Gray with Lines,* by Antoni Tapies (Spain) 1961

You were bewitching, with those dark eyes boring through the smoke to find me, that tousled head of steely blue black tresses. The only time we'd ever gone for lunch, I watched in fascination as you shook the pepper methodically, for a long time, fully blanketing your clam chowder. I liked quite a bit myself, on easy-over eggs, when the yolk was warm and wobbling over sliced tomatoes. The sharp, woodsy scent rose up over the bitter warmth of my coffee, and I asked you for a spoonful.

It's good for what ails you, I conceded, wiping small flecks of piperidine from my mouth with a napkin and hoping there were none in my teeth. It is indeed, you said. The vanadium helps you absorb more nutrients from the rest of the meal. This small shared fire wasn't enough, of course. I could not even woo you with foodie foofaraw- you would effortlessly outdo me. Still, I followed your cooking spiels constantly ever after on Youtube. I was addicted, and now I put pepper on everything.

The Astronomer

after *Conversations with God*, by Jan Matejko (Poland) 1873

Imagine you up on the highest rooftop, chin perched on the hook of the moon. You put your eye into long gleaming tube and everything turns to silver stone. You reach out, wave your hands, dip into the planetary pools, gin rings circling the other worlds. You make notes, sketch out the signs. Your mind is running in the distance, turning cartwheels through time. Imagine, chipping a rock or dirt with your nail, holding it tight until you languish, bringing meteors home with you after a long night's work.

The Broken Column

"My painting carries with it the message of pain."

Frida Kahlo

A tale of two Fridas, one with heart rooted in Mexico, hands and head like wild birds: expansive and free.

One Frida, chained by pain and accident and broken bones, cursed before birth to crutches, a wheelchair, and the small bed in the room upstairs.

She watches the garden from up in the window of her studio, how her husband, Diego, keeps touching her sister's arm with his grubby paws. Those hands that have turned rubble to mural, changed the very fate of the nation, but can't resist the sweetness of unbroken female flesh.

The other Frida often paints the heart, not with flowers or cute little wings or holy flames, but veins and valves and ventricles, pumping fast and hard, fighting for life the way she always has.

Turquoise

after *Untitled (Blue Divided by Blue),* by Mark Rothko (USA, b. Latvia) 1966

Once when we reached the west coast and the sea was a turquoise expanse under the falling neon orb of the sun, I wanted you to drink me down. You leaned in to kiss me, but it felt like you were distracted and far away. And then you said, do you ever think of it? Do you? Do you ever dream of drowning?

Silent Sky

after *Nightfall 2,* by Alison Britton-Patterson (USA) contemporary

The hidden place, in full view. Red cliffs above. Teal, peeling, frayed against the day's blue. You could follow the sound of the silence to find her, or take your bike down the dirt road and park it where the daisies would watch over it. We would scramble up a brick pile and crawl through the window, hearts drumming in the broken light. There were tarps spread across barrels and bags of fertilizer and feed; we imagined they might shroud the bodies of all those missing girls in the news. In the loft, stars and spiders spilled through the missing beams, and we could almost touch the moon. We would unwrap pickle sandwiches and wait for UFOs. Split a carton of chocolate milk. Later, Cranberry Vodka coolers and your guitar. We tried kissing then, and found it awkward. It has been eighteen years since you got sick and had to go. Sometimes I go back, wander under the winding canyon sprawl, to our hiding place. I'm still looking for you there.

Plague

after *Art is Trash,* by Francisco de Pajaro (Spain) contemporary

Barcelona. We saw God, in Gaudi. We ate French pastries, later, in the old quarter, and looked at graffiti art, Basquiat-esque paintings, in a few galleries I wanted to visit. Down by the boats, the humidity turned dusty rose, the sky broken by jolting, swooping bats. We dipped our fingertips in melted butter and crabs, and polished off a carafe of vino tinto.

Now the church is closed, and the city is empty of pilgrims. Only the hospitals and the morgues are full. Corona did not wait a year to curse the place. What has become of all those donut peaches with plummy innards, of the pebbly green olives we sucked to the bones?

Things You Should Know About Me

after *Moonlight Masquerade,* by Konstantin Somov (Russia) before 1939

I am a parade of disguises- first I play your lover, then the friend. I can convince you that I'm listening when I need something from you. But I'm not a good liar when I'm afraid, which is most of the time. I look solid but I'm just a precarious arrangement of found pottery and caulking. I always wear blue and white and iron everything, from socks to dishtowels. I'm the odd one out who loves the molasses taffy leftovers from Halloween- I will gladly trade my Aero bars and Smarties. But I will steal when you're not looking, anything you've touched that I can keep.

Like a Prayer

after milagro-covered crosses, folk art (Mexico) contemporary

If I could run away, it would be Mexico, it would be the gilt-edged altars and all those little brass legs. I would spill a sea of milagros at a shrine just to see you if it would summon you. I imagine you'd come running, hear my prayers, know I was there, but there was no real way to tell you. You were the feathers I had covered with earth the last time I was down there. You transformed to celluloid, to plaster mask with orange and purple chrysanthemums in November. You were a bloom in humid air, close, clingy, covered in stamens and meteors. I asked permission to step across the threshold. You didn't know what you were in for, and neither did I.

Spring

after *Lovers,* by Pierre-Auguste Renoir (France) 1875

My man has warm hands and he's ticklish. You can draw a line from his palm to the tender bend inside his elbow, but he won't stay still. He will wriggle, and giggle, and the small silver tufts to either side of his wife beater will shyly curl, tumbling to nipple, smugly nubbing the fabric blend. My man lets me into his mouth, yields that slick slug of tongue to my entry. Breathes his life back into me. My man soaks a cloth in brook water and champagne, presses it to my lips when I am thirsty. He traces everything I've given him, told him, on the steel strings of his guitar. He bands me in garlands of fluffy yellow flowers, sings to me in the dark about rivers and all the things that I've forgotten.

Haunt

after *Santa Anita Village,* by William Wray (USA) contemporary

Late at night, awake, in wait for you. I knew you weren't coming, I knew you couldn't, wouldn't, didn't; I knew you were way past all this. I knew you were long gone. But I waited still. I grew old.

The Bird Man

after *The Healer,* by Rene Magritte (Belgium) 1967

His hat was an intricate lattice of earth and sand coloured arrow cane palm leaves that kept the sun off his shoulders. He had rings in his nose and stripes lining his face. Inside the bird cage where his heart used to be, there was a chess board, diamond squares dancing backwards and emptying a ballroom of pawns and horses into the sea. His glass eyes seemed to smile as I approached, so I reached out, took a small strange key from his outstretched hand. There was a mechanical, clanking sound then, as if someone had put a coin into the slot of an old carnival game, a clattering of machinery folding in on itself. I slid the small key into my pocket, and everything disappeared in a thin plume of smoke. All that was left- a few quetzal feathers, drifting towards the floor.

Riverbank

Two Nudes, by Marcel Duchamp (France) 1910

The brunette and the redhead are both naked, lollygagging in a tangle of murky vines. The carrot top has a blank expression; she has no nipples. Her waist is cinched, angular, pinched by an invisible corset; her softness is reined in at the seams. The other is turned towards her and cannot see us here on the outskirts. If each woman is wishing for hands or feet or a tongue, it doesn't show. Bliss is an afternoon in the cool pond, oblivious to anyone looking, now, or in a hundred years.

Pappardelle

after vintage *Pasta Ambra* ad (Italy) details not known

The pot is rattling with heat on the stovetop, and the noodles are almost perfect. You juggle a few cherry tomatoes and a sharp knife expertly until they are small crimson slivers, and the plush meaty brine of the Cerignola olives will give gravitas to summery lemon and basil. You are, after all, the pappardelle princess. The time you added braised quail you won a cooking contest and went home with the judge's girlfriend- but that's a long story for another time. Tonight you have one of your headaches again, but you put on the bright red V-neck blouse that gives you luscious cleavage. You're doing your best. You have a bottle of something white and spicy chilling, too. You thought of doing a different bird braise, but a voice inside told you not to bother. It's been a few months since she noticed anything about you, and you can't help but think she's gone. For all you know, she's not coming home, tonight, or at all, but has run off, making meatballs with the ravioli queen.

Odd Job Jane

after Daria Petrilli (Italy) contemporary

Mission: to rid winter of imps and karakondzula. I had no idea what the sign meant, but I applied. I needed work. That was how I found myself hunting domovoi with page markers and highlighter. Until I began dismantling maps and old books that smelled like caraway and cabbage, I believed it was all imagination. After a few failed stakeouts, I turned in my first capture, handing my boss a djinn in an old apothecary bottle. *I thought these were only stories,* I said, pocketing my pay. He tossed my kill into the heap of history, all squirming bugaboos and scuddling things, barely looking up. *You'd be surprised,* he said.

The Daffodil Hunter

after *Fury,* by Francis Bacon (Ireland) 1944

"I lived through the revolutionary Irish movement, Sinn Fein and the wars, Hiroshima, Hitler and the death camps and daily violence that I've experienced all my life. And after all that they want me to paint bunches of pink flowers ..." Francis Bacon

Too much Wordsworth, everything dancing and yellow. No more beauty and bliss. Too much happiness. No winds of March, please, this. These happy hearts, tease, all pleasure and petals, too much. The streets of Johannesburg are a river of sweat and soot. Beirut is drowning in blood. Kiev in tatters. No more fluttering, no more breeze jazz, please. A jar full, hunted flowers, on the shelf of a friend. He pursues plastic promises pinned against disease, but where and if and when? Bright butter bursting through the earth when winter ends, emblem of hope and faith and it depends.

The Yaffle

after *Jay, Green Woodpecker, Pigeons, and Redstart,* by Francis Barlow (UK) 1650

The green-feathered redhead perched atop of tombstone moss sounded lonesome, but you said he was laughing. It was the graveyard where nobody goes, an unholy boneyard for debtors and pirates, now inhabited by vultures and starving dogs. I thought it was beautiful, overgrown with vines and spirits sprawling towards the black bog on the horizon. You were sure it was bad juju and wanted to make our way back to the inn. If I knew already that was always how it was, and how it would be, I didn't say so yet. I was still hopeful, in those days, that there was a place for me among the living. You were already growing tired of all the birdwatching. You knew I was only chasing ghosts.

Wildfire

for Edmonia Lewis, whose Ojibwe name was Wildfire

"M. Edmonia Lewis is a Black girl sent by subscription to Italy having displayed great talents as a sculptor." inscription on Edmonia Lewis's passport application, 1865

Minnehaha, in marble. Molded by wildfire, by long dark fingers. She carved and cut, coaxed life from granite so skillfully that Michelangelo would marvel. She brought Shakespeare's Queen of Egypt to life, three thousand pounds of alabaster, ruler of Africa, white as snow. The artist, a mere woman, and red and black as earth. The massive statue was stuffed into storage, later purchased by a dandy gambler. He wanted a gravestone for his racehorse, Cleopatra.

"The land of liberty had no room for a colored sculptor," said Edmonia, gone to Rome. She studied and worked, softening stone, igniting bone. The Italians saw her fire.

The Americans lynched her before she got away, leaving her for dead in an Ohio field. They charged her for poisoning two boys at school, dragging her into court the same way they dragged women to the pyre some centuries before. She was acquitted, then charged for stealing paints and plaster, but her hands were still clean.

Forever Free, an 1867 statue, her victory, a monument to abolition. Her proclamation of emancipation.

Lamentation for the Empty Fields

after The Crucified Land, by Alexander Hogue (USA) 1939

The fallows have nothing left to yield- they are valleys of dry bones.
The spindly limbs of withered trees shake their empty hands at the sky.
The grain grasses are waving scarecrows. How dare you?

Temple

after *BAPS Shri Swaminarayan Mandir,* Brampton Ontario

"Come on, come on, come on, come on, let me into your temple..." Jane Siberry

We were drinking Carmenere from the two surviving teacups in the set, the small blue Persian glasses without handles. Our tongues all purple like the Hindu gods. The image made me turn to the Kali figurine, her eternal fury of creation and destruction on guard in the dry soil of my cactus planter. Well, you know nothing of my private sacrifices, those tiny tears at the seams where I am stitched together, and just the same, I couldn't name what you have buried if I tried. On the eve of my secrets, I went to that alabaster temple, the one with no nails. The deva and devi surrounded me, white witnesses, as if they had always been waiting there for me to find them. I took off my shoes, held out my hands. Confessed what I was about to give away, or give back, what I would never get back. I surrendered my second chances. Made peace with all that regret before it showed its face. Chose a small joss from the gift shop, worried it in my palm like a polished stone.

Four Seasons

after *Four Seasons,* by Alphonse Mucha (Czechia) 1900

Winter

A long December, and frost has swallowed the mirror shores. You have not received my letters- I destroyed them all.

Spring

Heart thaws with the sun and the bright and breezy bobbing dance of tulips. I run back for you, through meadows and mud puddles.

Summer

The early moon shelters the bullfrog's bellow, serenading the sticky heat of the gloaming. We had our moments, a few more of them.

Autumn

September falls later than usual this year, returning dead leaves to earth just before the snow.

Hopscotch

"Antoni Tapies is my very favorite artist, his work touches something in me I can't explain."

Maggie Attenborrow, Youtube comments

1. In Mexico City, my first face to face encounter with Tapies.

A massive wall of burnt sienna, paint dark as loam.

2. A void full of dreams. Sigils and signs. Sticks and stones.

3. His work is everywhere before you know his name:

- Fresh cement, poured, scarred soon after by passing teens.

-A crumbling wall under a bridge.

-The bumpy terrain of dried gum wads on the underside of an old snooker table.

-Spilled blood on kitchen linoleum after the slip of a knife.

-The writing on the wall.

Ennui

after *Young Boy Feeding Rabbits,* by John Bradley (USA, b. England) 1831

In the long gloaming, the boy wanders the grounds behind the pines, waiting for the world outside the walls. Only the rabbits can find him, crepuscular critters with the moon on the tips of their tongues.

Milk

after Agnes Martin (Canada)1912-2004

1. It is how I was able to find you, in layers.

2. Arsenic, antimony: under pure night, poison.

3. Tall tales, spinning. White lies, unravelling.

4. I dreamed of prairie summers, of seven swans lost to the sea in the blinding light of fields of wheat.

5. Salt cellars, silver spoons, pale round pebbles. Your little altars on white glass.

6. You were all teeth: your tongue a mystery behind those marmoreal pearly gates.

7. Heart laid bare. Our unrequited search for simplicity, honesty, milk.

Our Lady of Laughter

after *Come Holy Spirit,* by Lance Brown (USA) contemporary

I was at the laughing church in Toronto, where they said there had been some kind of miracle of mirth. My hometown wasn't especially known for its miracles, so I chomped back my defiance and let my curiosity lead me there. There was nothing funny but everything was friendly, too much so. My guarded worship wasn't used to swirling ribbons and toe slippers, to jolting jigs and weeping on the floor. My girlfriend poked me. *I want to know if it feels different if I pray with my hands in the air,* she said, just loudly enough that I could hear her in the cacophony of wailing and wonder. She shot her arms upwards, waved them as if we were at a Bon Jovi concert. *It does,* she said. *It does!* I put my hands up, too, wiggled my pinkies in the glow of Abraham. Held my hope up to heaven, waiting to be touched or blessed.

Quarantine

after *Family Life During a Pandemic,* by Leif Larson (USA)
2020

You put a chicken in the oven, cover it in spices, wait for the fat to
broil. The cumin catches fire, the cinnamon and jerk melt to incense.
How many more birds will wait for you? You have bought yourself a
month or two, towers of tuna, bread and butter pickles, a whole row of
Chardonnay. These will, of course, only buy time. This is love in the
time of corona, love tucked behind the meat in the fridge, love, raw and
sorry and strange where only the falling canyon shadows can reach it.
You are already rolling out under the pasta and the playlists. There are
two unbroken weeks of toilet paper ahead, but nothing else is certain.
The television is tired. It's the first pandemic cushioned by Netflix and
legal marijuana, but no *Sherlock*, no black mirrors, no rituals in the
damn red earth, can tame the taste of terror between your teeth.

Gertrude

after *The Cat,* by Alberto Giacometti (Switzerland) 1951

Old Gertie was a spinster even as a kitten, when I was a kitten. She was bone thin and long and nervous but looked bossy. She was a gray tabby with a scaly skin disorder. She loved to swat the air for moths and starlings that weren't there. She exuded vague scents of urine and honeysuckle; she liked liverwurst and egg salad sandwiches. Like all great aunts, she lived forever, getting older and older and still showing up at funerals and weddings. She lived so long, she might still be there now.

An Important Thing I Learned From Leonard Cohen

after *Bath,* by Leonard Cohen (Canada) 2008

1. There's sex in everything.

2. Not in the ubiquitous grunting and groaning, or at least, least of all, there.

3. Poetry is sex.

4. There's sex in everything. That's how the life gets in.

Cold Comfort

after *Sun in Parlour,* by Vilhelm Hammershoi (Denmark) 1901

If God watching you was supposed to give some comfort, well, it didn't. You could never shake the uneasy feeling that there was someone in the house.

Bittersweet

after *Redhead Falling Down Stairs,* by Antonio Santin (USA) contemporary

It was never easy going back. The gloom was as thick as the damask drapery, and their enormous dusty tassels seemed symbolic somehow, ornamental bonds. The whole house smelled of chocolate and oranges. Bitterness polished in culinary perfume like a scarred banister salvaged by lemon oil. Descending those curlicue stairs, you saw more than your reflection in the grand gilt mirror that had hung there since World War One. In the desilvering ripples, the redhead was always floating down after you, the girl with no eyes and fire for hair.

Chanterelle

after *Female Nude,* by Joaquin Sorolla (Spain) 1886

The altars were heaped with flowers and the air was humid with mango perfume. I felt like my hands were dissolving in warm waves when you touched them. The curves of you, your goddess softness. All of my doubts fell away. We were dancing while still and silent but I could hear the music, melodies and reverberations rolling in from the dark edges of time. It was almost as if there was no one else there. Accordion organdy, saffron yellow. The whole room was a lantern.

A Dance with the Devil

after *The Aliados Crew in Botas Picudas, Dance Off at Mesquit Rodeo*, by Dario Lopez-Mills (Mexico) 2011

The start of the sound, Sunday salsa in the square. The icy xocoatl is my only relief from the oppressive blaze of the sun, but the locals don't seem to notice or mind. No one else sees the devil, either, but there he is, in blazing polyester, head to toe and skin tight. His feet are flamboyant in ridiculous *botas picudas*, pointy red boots so long they look like skis.

I catch the eye of the butcher as the carousel of couples spins past. His joyous face is round and ruddy, his chubby fingers sprawled across the back rolls of his dancing queen. A toothy grin invites me to step into the circle. But my dance card is full. All the bobbing, jumping faces flash by, jovial jowls, sky wide smiles, even as the devil lurks there in the shadows. He'll find his way over to me. He always does.

Closing Time

after *The Bohemians,* by Christian Krohg (Norway) 1885

I'm just a baby, but won't know it for another twenty years. I'm loud and brash to cover up the lost and shy. I'm on a patio on Davie Street with a new friend in my new city. The photographer. He is long and thin and orange. He takes photos of weird mannequins and gum wads on sidewalks. I yell at him for ordering lamb shish kabob, tell him he is a murderer and he will drop dead of jammed arteries before we get to know each other. He is more shy, and even more damaged than I am. But he is ten years older and has lived enough to laugh it off. He likes me anyways. We both have a penchant for oddities and for characters. We both love the poetry we find in the cracks. We both love Leonard Cohen. And I'm not the first vegan he has met in Vancouver.

Code of Silence

after *Self Portrait,* by Helene Schjerfbeck (Finland) 1915

The sister hasn't spoken in months, you say. More than that, actually, nearly a year. Things were just going along and then one day, she stopped talking. At first you thought she was playing some messed up kind of trick that you weren't getting. Then you thought it was a protest. Sometimes she would write something down in the little notebook she'd started carrying around. But there would just be a few cryptic words like "the broken heart of Mexico" or "before they turn the summer into dust." It took some figuring but eventually you caught on that these were snippets of song lyrics. Nothing in her own words, not even on paper.

Late Lunch

after *Picnic V*, by Fernando Botero (Colombia) 1990s?

It's still too warm for October, and the trees are reluctant to give up their green for gold. You have spread out a cloth covered in neon poppies, a brisk pop art splotch in the middle of the orchard clearing. I ceremoniously unpack a lemon, Parmesan heels, a blooming round of sourdough. The requisite picnic Burgundy is already uncorked. You hesitate a second, working out the decorum with a few woodpeckers and wasps before tilting it straight up to your mouth. When I take my turn it's like being kissed. The world is covered in apples.

Consolation

after *Cocaine,* by Jan Kamyk (Poland) 2019

And what if the love of your life was a drug, you ask us as we wait, your razor deftly working the mirror. If the most transcendent place you'd ever been hallowed was an illusion of dopamine? How the hollow in your head was nearly holy once you'd touched straw to synapse, blown blinkers on a powder's small stigmata. Well, if I ever still talk about addiction as if it was a terrible love story, that's exactly what it was.

Marooned

after Gertrude Abercrombie (USA) 1909-1977

In the scattered, silver sparks on the way back from the sea, I gather spilled secrets, lonesome emeralds, malachite, like stars, like seeds. In the soft matrix of the horizon line, a sign: you are half-man, half-moon, and half of what's left of me.

Dark Horse

after *Horse Frightened by Lightning,* by Eugene Delacroix (Spain)
1824

Something about horses, something about their warm and fluid grace,
these giants, dinosaurs, as strong and sleek as dancers. something fierce
and elegant. Something about morning, something clean and bright and
fresh, something hopeful and ready. Something about the leathery musk
of latherin, something about the rhythmic tock tick of hoof-clops, that
equine canter its own kind of heartbeat. Something about the redheads,
those rusty chestnut steeds glowing against the grass like polished
cherries. Something about their sloe-eyed beauty. Something about the
blondes, caramel palominos first to flirt, all gallop and giggly whinny.
Something about night, something about white, the white ones, the moon
mares, their alabaster flares, luminescent in midnight. How they are
easily spooked, how they can always tell a coming storm.

Habanero

after *Laid Table*, by Nicolaes Gillis (Netherlands) 1611

There you are again, the way you show up every few years, at the canape table with a tumbler to the brim. You rifle past a fragrant aging cheddar, pilfer the final smear of habanero marmalade on a gherkin. You are juggling an armload of Lydia Davis and I know we are thinking the same thing: how satisfying and tactile the heft of that book, substantial and wide in inches but still floating and airy, like an Aero bar. We will mull the appeal of her brevity even as I long for more adjectives, for words that flirt or float instead of thudding so purposefully across the page, but if I said so, there will be withering glares, as if I was committing an indiscretion, as if I had double dipped the blue corn crisp I was nibbling on so nervously. Well, you were as scrawny and nervous as a cricket when we first fell into each other on a chess board dance floor. It was a lifetime ago, it was all Leonard Cohen and the Cocteau Twins and you had four pinprick sapphires festering in the top tier of cartilage of your ear. We were looking for love in the time of corrosion, seeking God at in the speakeasies and dives. How time flies. How everything changes, and yet, remains the same. In two more pakoras and a wedge of Leicester Red you will look up, see me waiting for you.

Masquerade

after *Masquerade,* by Mariano Fortuny (Spain) 1868

We have forgotten the boats of Venice and the masked men that followed us later that year, through the mist and the snaking streets of Vienna. If it was a dream, you don't remember it. Oh, we all have masks, mine was soft blue leather, cuffed like a bearded lizard, a puff dragon. I held it in front of me and peered through it, revelled in the masquerade. If it was hard to find love in those alleys, I have no one else to blame. I was running from God through the back streets, running to hide from your game.

Missing

after *Self-Portrait in Semi-Abstract Style*, by Sylvia Plath (USA)
1952

I find *Ariel*, I find her on the floor in the corner of my room, under an ashtray, under the weight of all these words. My mother calls: her voice is hollow and dizzy, with the latest. She is missing again, but so am I. I do not know where to run, where to turn, where to land. I do not know where to find her, I do not know where I am.

Night Swimming

after *Bright Light at Russel's Corners,* by George Ault (USA) 1946

The wine is cold and clear on this river. The taste of soil, and salt. You flapped and floundered with the oars when the waves threatened higher than mere ripples; you always could see danger in the deep when I was blind. My eyes are knives, now, under ice, and yours are blooming blood. Is the night still what it claims to be, a void and distant sorrow?

White Mare

after Gertrude Abercrombie (USA) 1909-1977

You are alone, again, a solitary coral bloom in deserted midnight. The moon follows you everywhere, a fingernail of frost cutting open your sky. You walk through walls and stand at the edge of the night, overlooking long lanes of empty houses. There is a ladder propped against a bare branch and you do not know where it goes. You stare back at an owl that lands in the tree above you. You cannot read his secrets, but you are no longer afraid of everything. The bird hoots, then turns into a mirror, and a black cat is your reflection. You raise one arm, wave it, claiming the kingdom as your own. A white mare appears. You mount her in silence, knowing you will go with her, without question: wherever she leads you is your way home.

Sinister Harvest

after Zdislaw Beksinski (Poland) 1929-2005

It arrived in the shape of a dream, the last bird, the last winged thing in the godforsaken village. Every other thing that breathed had already gone, trailing fins and feathers through the flames and fog, disappearing beyond the waves and the flowers. We, too, were already half vanished. If part of me remained, it was only my morbid curiosity. The end of the world, that kind of thing: I had to see it for myself.

Midnight Train

after *Horse and Train*, by Alex Colville (Canada) 1950

Well, you had a cat that looked like Grace Jones, all crazy cheekbones and hard angles. Midnight coat and hungry eyes. You were half wild yourself, exactly as you'd warned me. If I didn't believe you at first, then, yes, I guess, I confess, I was impressed or maybe fooled by the still waters and forgot how deep they run in mirrors. I was all about glow and spectacle but even so, only looking for a safe space to land. You were a slower simmer than cheap glitter and I should have known better. You told me straight up, *it ain't me, babe,* and I followed anyways. And so, now I know. How I would always find the undertow or the oncoming train, even if you were the dark horse I never saw coming.

Violets

after *Violets,* by Pauline Powell Burns (USA) 1890

The brightest star in the state, wrote one critic of her music. Young, gifted, and black. Great granddaughter of a Jefferson slave, and her grandmother belonged to someone else. Still a tender teen, Pauline was performing piano, exhibiting her paintings. Champagne and oysters, watery nasturtiums. Tuberculosis erased it all by forty. Only a few small canvases remain, and nothing of her music. Still, for a spark, she was seen and heard. Her beautiful photograph a ghost of history. She is dissolving to dust, a sprig of fading violets.

Butter

after *Mound of Butter,* by Antoin Vollon (France) 1875

Stubby fingers, pinching, pulling. Digging down to dough. I see stars. The eggs are still warm from the hens. I wanted to take you there in the coop, all that bossy and clucking fecundity in salt and straw. You blink twice, turn sideways, every time I catch your eye. Soda, you snap your fingers at the carton. Sugar, you say next, taking it from me, but holding back in your pour. The air is dense and saccharine from bananas. I fly back in time, to a Minnesota trailer. Prom gone wrong. I emptied all my tears into your cupcake tins because someone didn't know I was alive. What does it matter now? When here, when this. Truth be told, I forget who it was.

Smoke Signals

after *King's Noodles,* by Peter Harris (Canada) contemporary

When was the moment I first knew I would lose you? About eight weeks after we'd met, standing before you at the altar. The French horn sounding "Endless Love." The bridal march felt like a funeral. *There's something I've been meaning to tell you,* you'd said to me in the taxi on the way there. I still don't know what it was.

Pageant

after *Miss Chatelaine*, by Suzy Lake (Canada) 1973

The future Miss Chatelaine daubs a final explosion of glassine goo on her lower pout and declares herself battle ready. Glowering from her throne of cast and crutches, Maude, her injured sister, records the monumental transformation in her diary. *She glows, she gleams, a jewel among beauty queens.* She pauses, then crosses a line through her prose. *More like an ad for dish soap,* she thinks, as Celie flounces out into the pageant pandemonium in a cloud of imposter Obsession.

Silent Night

after *Moonlight*, by Helen McNicoll (Canada) 1905

The soundless sky speaks loudest; the silent moon meanders over marsh and into sky. Helen hears in violet, in brushstroke bulrush smudges, lush and viridescent in the dusk.

Apocalypse

after Kay Sage (USA) 1898-1963

*"I have said all that I have to say. There is nothing left for me
to do but scream."*

Kay Sage

Apocalypse then, now, and how Kafka-esque her metamorphosis.
The barren terrain, destitute, bleak. Her post-industrial cities span the
scars of the planets. Where nothing is left alive. Not even love. Kay
takes her death like she takes her whisky: straight up, and self-inflicted.
Unsentimental. Shot to the heart.

Jalopy

after *Self Portrait in the Green Bugatti,* by Tamara de Lempicka (Poland) 1929

Some men are Porsches. Sleek and silver, fine and riche, over the top, on top. Well-oiled machines. Some are folksy, vans, Volkswagons, all rusty authenticity, flowery, free loving. Some guys are shy, slim, expensive, Audi, all feline Russian Blue. Some are hot blooded, top down, skylight seekers soaring through the sun. I'm looking for the one who painted polka dots on his jalopy at a demolition derby, proudly wore the runner up ribbon in his dungaree bib. It's the tried and true, the dilapidated denim driver that does it for me. The soda sweet simplicity, hands up, hands down, crumpled hunk of burning love.

The Game of Keys

after Gertrude Abercrombie (USA) 1909-1977

In the rainy city before dawn, two shrouded women in the garden of the city square. They stand guard on either side of the chess table. One holds an hour glass in her hand, and the other holds the upside down corpse of a small bird. They sense your presence and lift their faces: neither of them have eyes.

The woman under a white cloud touches the shank of a rusty key, pushes it forward several squares toward the centre of the board. She lifts her hand skyward, first and last finger touching, like a mysterious mudra.

The other pulls a deep red ribbon and then a narrow key from her mouth. She places it in the row closest to her. She briefly touches one thumb to both ears, then sways the fallen sparrow over the game like a macabre pendulum. An owl asleep on a barren branch stirs, then swoops, taking something from a chalice in the middle of the board.

A black cat moves from the shadows into the game. There is a tiny silver key at her throat. The pale wedge of moon left over from the night dissolves against the lightening sky.

Vanishing

after *Spirit of the Aquifer,* by Marsha Reeves (USA) contemporary

A cloudless sky, rain soft as skin. This is how I bury you, at the edge of the old aquifer, tangled in snowdrops and honeysuckle. You will be safe here, honey, no one will look for you, no one will know what you have done.

The Rope Artist

after *Cross My Heart,* by Caroline Bacher (Canada) 2021

It is his hands that bound me first, the intricate way the strange slender fingers skated along the seams, how they seemed to tangle at the button eye, intent in concentration, then come undone, dancing down to spool and skein. I watched him work the fabric, furrowing, smoothing, the fine needle sliver through satin ribboning up and down my spine. I had never been tied down, or tied up, but there I was, tethered by the tips of his thumbs and the bead of sweat on his upper lip as if by a red silk cord. I paid for the garment repairs, saved his name on the slip, and eventually went back with an invitation. Later, he would caress the arch of my foot before binding it against the other, weave me in shibari in a position of prayer. His hands worked the spaces between the skin and the rope, tenderly from tip to toe, as if I was a treasure.

Magnolia

after *Magnolia Tree,* by Dan Cooper (USA) contemporary

Pink Patsy's throne was her porch, where she roosted like a proud poodle through the better part of a century. She was all pretty pastry and puffball in oodles of swaddled satins and mega bijoux, with cloudward curls as epic as her jewels. Her communal vat of ice cubes and iced tea was legendary among heat-struck fieldhands and thirsty children alike: there was more gin than lemon or sugar, and we fished out ice with silver tongs that looked like chicken feet. They said she kept a tiny pearl pistol in her pom-pom mules, and she only used it once.

About the Author

Canada's Lorette C. Luzajic writes, writes about, edits, publishes, and teaches prose poetry and flash fiction, most often ekphrastic. She has a degree in journalism but went down a more creative path. Obsessed with art history, she views art as a way for people to connect with others in different times, places, and idea frameworks. She fuels her writing and her own visual art on this enchantment. (Lorette is an "award-winning, internationally exhibited artist with collectors in 30 countries.) She is also the founder and editor of *The Ekphrastic Review,* the flagship journal of literature inspired by art.

Lorette's stories and prose poems have appeared in hundreds of journals, magazines, and anthologies. Her recent books include *Salt* (Cyberwit Books), *Pretty Time Machine,* and *Winter in June* (Mixed Up Media Books). Lorette's small stories placed recently as short list finalist in the Bath Flash Fiction Awards, longlist in the Furious Fiction Australia Awards, and first place in a *MacQueen's Quinterly* contest. She has been nominated four times each for the Pushcart Prize and Best of the Net, as well as twice for Best Small Fictions and three times for Best Microfictions.

Lorette's other passions include collecting assorted oddments and artifacts, archeology and ancient cultures, eccentrics, artisan rings, silver, beads, blues music, orange cats, photography, world masks, flamenco, folk horror, Mediterranean cooking, and everything about Mexico.

Acknowledgements

Thank you to the Ontario Arts Council for their support for the writing of these prose poems and microfictions.

Thank you to *Flash Boulevard* for nominating "The Bird Man" for *Best Microfictions*.

Thank you to *The Ilanot Review* for nominating "The Rope Artist" for *Best Microfictions*.

Thank you to the fine literary journals who first published some of these works.

Credits in order of poem's appearance in this collection.

"Las Ramblas" first appeared in *MacQueen's Quinterly*.

"The Broken Column" first appeared in *Indelible*.

"Silent Sky" first appeared in *Subterranean Blues*.

"The Bird Man" first appeared in *Flash Boulevard*.

"Pappardelle" first appeared in *Flash Boulevard*.

"Odd Job Jane" first appeared in *New Flash Fiction Review*.

"Wildfire" first appeared in *Indelible*.

"Lamentation for the Empty Fields" first appeared in *Canto Planetario*, an anthology edited by Carlos Javier Jarquin.

"Temple" first appeared in *Book of Matches*.

"Four Seasons" first appeared in *MacQueen's Quinterly*.

"Hopscotch" first appeared in *MacQueen's Quinterly*.

"Milk" first appeared in *Indelible.*

"Bittersweet" first appeared in *New Flash Fiction Review.*

"A Dance with the Devil" first appeared in *New Flash Fiction Review.*

"White Mare" first appeared in *Scapegoat.*

"Sinister Harvest" first appeared in *Friday Flash Fiction.*

"Midnight Train" first appeared in *Macqueen's Quinterly.*

"Violets" first appeared in *Indelible.*

"Butter" first appeared in *The Bird Seed.*

"Smoke Signals" first appeared in *Six Sentences.*

"Pageant" first appeared in *Microfiction Mondays Magazine.*

"Silent Night" first appeared in *Trouvaille Review.*

"Apocalypse" first appeared in *Rye Whiskey Review.*

"Jalopy" first appeared in *Blue Pepper Journal.*

"Game of Keys" first appeared in *Flash Boulevard.*

"The Rope Artist" first appeared in *The Ilanot Review.*

"Magnolia" first appeared in *A Story in 100 Words.*

9 789395 224611